CLASSIC POETRY FOR DOGS

CLASSIC POETRY FOR DOGS

WHY DO I CHASE THEE

from **ELIZABETH BASSET BROWNING** & OTHER CANINE MASTERS

JESSICA SWAIM ★ ILLUSTRATED BY CHET PHILLIPS

GIBBS SMITH
TO ENRICH AND INSPIRE HUMANKIND

HOW DO I THANK THEE?
MARIANNE MCKIERNAN, TRACIE VAUGHN ZIMMER,
LISA WHEELER, CAROLINE STUTSON

18 17 16 15 14   5 4 3 2 1

Published by
Gibbs Smith
P.O. Box 667
Layton, Utah 84041

1.800.835.4993 orders
www.gibbs-smith.com

Designed by Katie Jennings Campbell
Printed and bound in China

Gibbs Smith books are printed on either recycled, 100% post-consumer waste, FSC-certified papers or on paper produced from sustainable PEFC-certified forest/controlled wood source. Learn more at www.pefc.org.

Library of Congress Cataloging-in-Publication Data

Swaim, Jessica.
  Classic poetry for dogs : why do I chase thee / Jessica Swaim ; illustrations by Chet Phillips. — First edition.
    pages cm
  ISBN 978-1-4236-3554-3
  1. Dogs—Poetry. 2. Humorous poetry, American. I. Phillips, Chet, illustrator. II. Title.
  PS3619.W345C57 2014
  811'.6—dc23
                    2013029139

CONTENTS

BARKING TO THE BEAT

Ever since the first wolf howled a haiku at the moon, canines have expressed their innermost thoughts and feelings in verse on such universal themes as puppy love, fleas, and the trauma of the spay/neuter experience. Oral tradition became transdogrified into print when an unknown mongrel scratched an early epic poem, *Beowoof,* on a scrap of material called poopyrus.

In the eons that followed, many ruff drafts were devoured by predators as well as by the poets themselves in the long, lonely periods between meals. However, thanks to the diligent transcription efforts of a few enlightened humans, some of the finest works of the canine masters survive today, from the sonnets of Shakespaw to the limericks of Dogden Dash and the villanelles of Droolin' Thomas.

Many modern day bards of the yard are prolific poets in their own right, although oblivious humans often mistake their poetry for a series of random arfs, bowwows, yips, yaps, and grrrs. These humans attempt to thwart free canine expression through the use of muzzles, squirt bottles, bark collars, and ubiquitous cries of "Shut up, you damn dog!" Sensitive souls who receive sudden, undeserved swats on the rump often suffer from bouts of depression and a form of creative constipation called "barker's block." Yet, despite ongoing attempts to curtail their work, contemporary canine poets continue to bark to the beat.

Sit. Stay. Read the work of these hounds of renown, faithfully preserved by

Yours truly,

Edna St. Vincent Sharpei, President
DEAD DOG POETS SOCIETY

WILLIAM SHAKESPAW

One of the most eloquent creatures to press paw to parchment, Shakespaw was born with a silver tongue. Hark, hark, the bard did bark! Born in Squatford, England, to strays of indeterminate lineage, he howled many sonnets but remains best known to the common cur for his plays, which include:

As You Lick It

Comedy of Terriers

Love's Labradors Lost

The Merry Wolves of Windsor

Taming of the Schnoodle

Julius Schnauzer

Romeo and Julie's Vet

Bite Us, Andronicus

SHALL I COMPARE THEE TO A STEAK FILLET?

Shall I compare thee to a steak fillet?

Thou art more flaccid and more apt to spoil;

Fat cows do graze on sweet alfalfa hay,

And nibble grass from rich organic soil,

Perchance with tender offspring at their sides;

They roam the range and breathe the freshen'd air,

Ere men with ill intent do smite their hides,

Then cook their flesh, well done or medium rare;

But thy aquatic diet makes thee frail,

From pucker'd lip to piteous dorsal fin,

With naught but bones betwixt thy head and tail,

And Death's cold kiss upon thy scaly skin;

So long as men may stoop to fill my dish,

I pray for steak, not thee, O slimy fish.

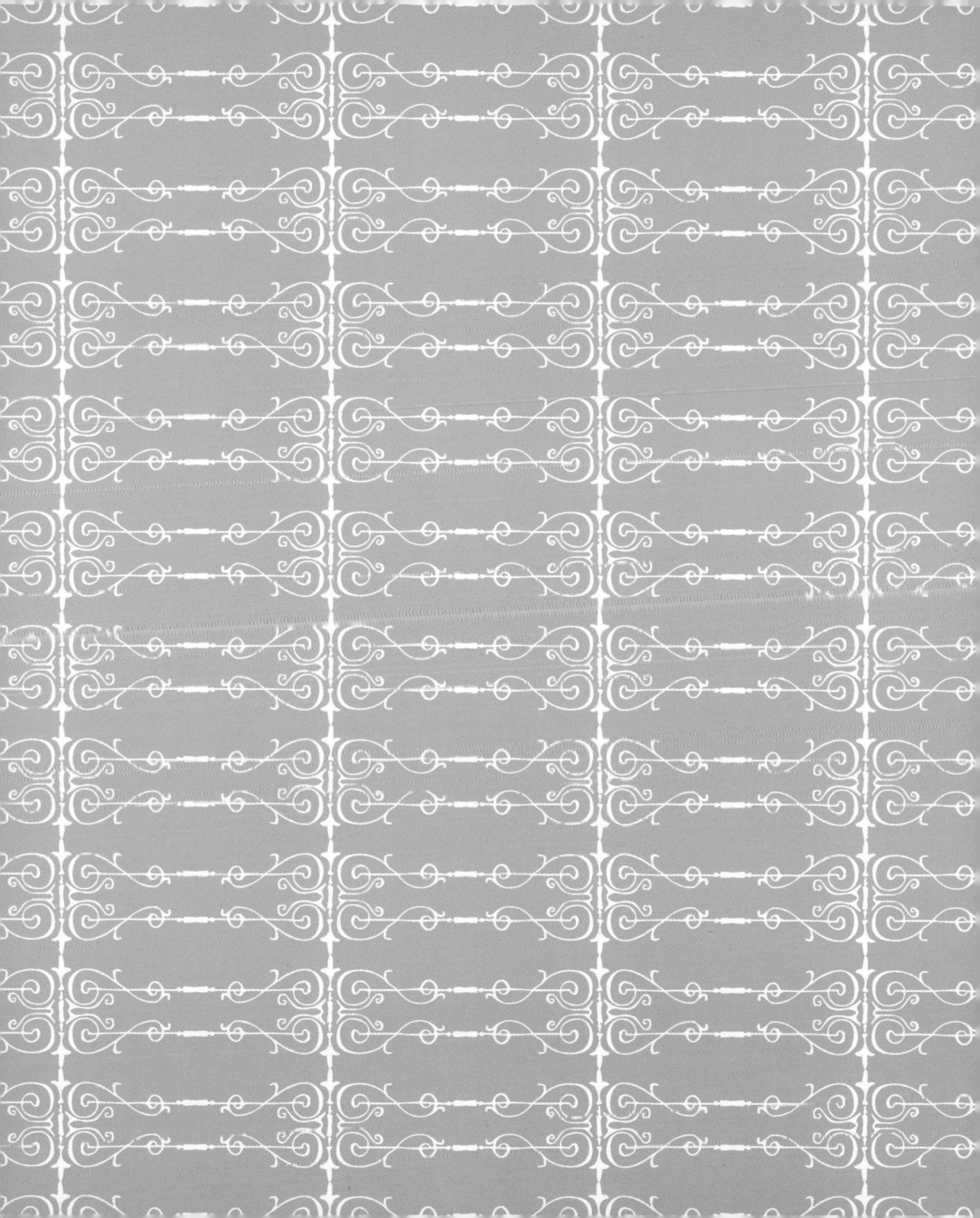

ELIZABETH BASSET BROWNING

Elizabeth Basset Browning is best remembered for her love poems, *Sonnets from the Portuguese Water Dog,* and for her romance with the dashing Rover Browning. During the couple's courtship, Elizabeth's father warned her that her fiancé was a gold digger. But, although Rover spent a lot of time displacing dirt, all he ever dug up were earthworms, hyacinth bulbs, and once a parakeet skeleton. The Brownings produced one pup, Rover Junior, who ran away from home soon after weaning, so embarrassed was he by his parents' constant humping.

WHY DO I CHASE THEE?

Why do I chase thee? Doggone it if I know.

I chase thee to the length and width and height

My teeth can reach, when bending to the right

And seeing thee behind me, wagging low.

I chase thee when the hours pass too slow

And Master needs to laugh, he's so uptight.

I chase thee gaily, dizzy with delight;

I chase thee roundly, as concentric circles grow.

I chase thee at a basset's bobbling pace,

With ears blown back and whirling dervish feet.

I chase thee in a timeless losing race

No dog can win—until I'm beat,

Trounced, whipped by thee, elusive tail!—then, in disgrace,

I start the chase again to make ends meet.

EDGAR ALLAN PUG

Best remembered for tales of terror like "The Pit Bull and the Pendulum," Edgar Allan Pug wrote with a plumed pen clutched in his tightly curled tail. His life was marked by ill health—ear mites, gum disease, and impacted anal glands.

At the age of seven, following a disturbing encounter with a talking raven, Pug went mad. Luckily, he kept on writing.

KITTY MCFLEA

It was many and many a moon ago,

In a kennel by the sea,

That a feline there lived, a calico,

By the name of Kitty McFlea;

And this feline she lived with no other aim

Than to claw and be clawed by me.

I was all nip and she was all scratch

In this kennel by the sea;

We started each day with a boxing match—

I and Miss Kitty McFlea.

She sucker punched (pow!) with a hiss and meow,

As she fought like Mohammad Ali . . .

'Til one fateful eventide, long ago,

From a branch of a cottonwood tree,

An owl swooped down and he grabbed ahold

Of the bellicose Kitty McFlea,

By the nape of her neck, though she struggled like heck,

And he bore her away from me.

As the cat disappeared, I admit that I cheered,

For my soul had at last been set free;

Now the owl never screams without bringing me dreams

Of the furball named Kitty McFlea.

Her unscheduled flight in the midst of our fight

Made it clear that the winner was me—yippee!—

And good riddance to Kitty McFlea!

In a kennel not far from the sea.

THE MAVEN

Once upon a table shiny, while I trembled, meek and whiny,

Over many a fume of chloroform too pungent to ignore,

While I slobbered, half-sedated, certain something grim awaited,

Sure enough, the vet I hated sauntered in and closed the door.

"Booster shot," I ruminated. "That is what this visit's for.

Just a shot, and nothing more."

While I let my thoughts thus wander, Doc examined me down yonder,

Leaving me not one bit fonder of the guy than theretofore.

Long he eyed me, clearly scheming, scalpel lifted, cruelly gleaming,

All the while, his face was beaming, dreaming of his evil chore.

Why, I wondered, had he whispered, just before he'd closed the door,

None too gently, "Nevermore."

So intent was he on snipping precious parts not meant for clipping,

That he scarcely heard me yipping, yipping as my flesh he tore.

Written there, upon his pocket, in red thread that seemed to mock it,

Such a name upon his smock—it shocked me to my very core.

Shocked was I, and stirred and shaken, shocked and shaken to my core,

Not to mention, very sore.

When at last the nightmare ended, gradually my stitches mended,

Due to tender care extended by the owner I adore.

Nonetheless, I felt quite bitter, for no stud was ever fitter,

And I'd only sired one litter, with a chocolate Labrador,

Heavy with our growing brood, she birthed them on a hardwood floor,

Six strong pups, and not one more.

Now that I am ten years older—hard of hearing, stiff of shoulder—

Memories grow ever colder of my youthful days of yore.

Rest assured I've not forgotten him who did the deed most rotten,

Leaving me with balls of cotton, at the fertile age of four,

Such a tragedy befell me, at the fertile age of four,

Love life ended evermore.

Long ago where once was shaven, on my rear is still engraven,

On my tender groin engraven, in that spot erstwhile so sore,

Words that cause my loins to quiver, heart to break, and spine to shiver,

Loud and long, I cried a river o'er that deed I yet deplore,

Words etched by the carving maven, craven surgeon I abhor—

"Neutered by Yul Suffermore."

ISSA SHIH TZU

The smallest and shaggiest of the Zen masters, Issa Shih Tzu grew up in the Pekingese province of Wag Low. By the age of six months, he had perfected the art of barking in sets of seventeen syllables. Although he rarely lost his serenity, the wee prodigy was known to foam at the mouth when forced to cuddle with strangers.

The wise Tzu's sayings include these:

"He who chases his own tail has a full circle moment."

"He who sniffs underwear soon pants."

"There is no problem that cannot be licked."

Winter landscape yearns
for random streaks of saffron—
urine on the snow.

Lift a hind leg high
as autumn wind is gusting;
tumble into fall.

Porcupine displays
his arsenal of needles:
acupuncture scam.

Boat ride ends at last.
My seasick heart rejoices,
frisbee in the sand.

Digging in the snow

I find last summer's woobie.

Time has not been kind.

Canine names abound

melodious as birdsong,

yet they call me Spud.

Wallow in the mud

'til master fills the washtub;

all good things must end.

HENRY WAGSWORTH LONGFELLOW

Proud to be one of literature's "horizontally gifted" dachshunds, Henry Wagsworth Longfellow wore the coarse beard typical of his wire-haired ancestors. In his hometown of Shortland, Maine, he waddled the streets with extraordinary dognity.

A rumor persists that the usually affable Longfellow once seized Walt Whippet by the throat after Whippet referred to him as *"der wiener rhymer."* Whippet later accused Longfellow of stretching the truth and insisted that he could never stoop that low.

LONGFELLOW'S PRIDE

Listen, my puppies, and you shall know
How your pappy fared at the Westminster show.
Not a week goes by that my thoughts don't stray
To the scene I caused on that winter day,
Just a little over a year ago.

I'd been schooled for weeks in the show-ring prance,
In the flowing gait and the steady stance,
For my master had but a single goal
And believed we had an excellent chance
To win the prize of a silver bowl.

I was lapping 'round on my leather lead,
The favored dog to take Best of Breed,
When a lovely chow just inside ring three

Began to bolt, and the Fates decreed

That her shortcut out should lead straight for me.

Farewell, my head and hello, my heart,

For I leaped the gate, which was none too smart.

Our honeymoon night was about to start.

The last I heard was the crowd's loud roar

As I chased my love out the double door.

The stars shone down and we took things slow.

That's all, my dears, that you need to know.

But, later on, we were vexed indeed

That a borzoi bitch took the Best of Breed

And a stuck-up spitz won the Best in Show.

When I brought her home as my chosen bride,

How my mistress laughed and my master cried!

By leaps and bounds, our devotion grew,

And a few weeks later, along came you,

Your mammy's joy and your pappy's pride.

It's bedtime now, so that's all I'll say

Of the strange events of that winter day.

But that's the story of why and how

You're one half wiener and one half chow,

Why Master failed to achieve his goal

And a stuck-up spitz won the silver bowl,

And why it is, to this very day,

Westminster tells me to stay away.

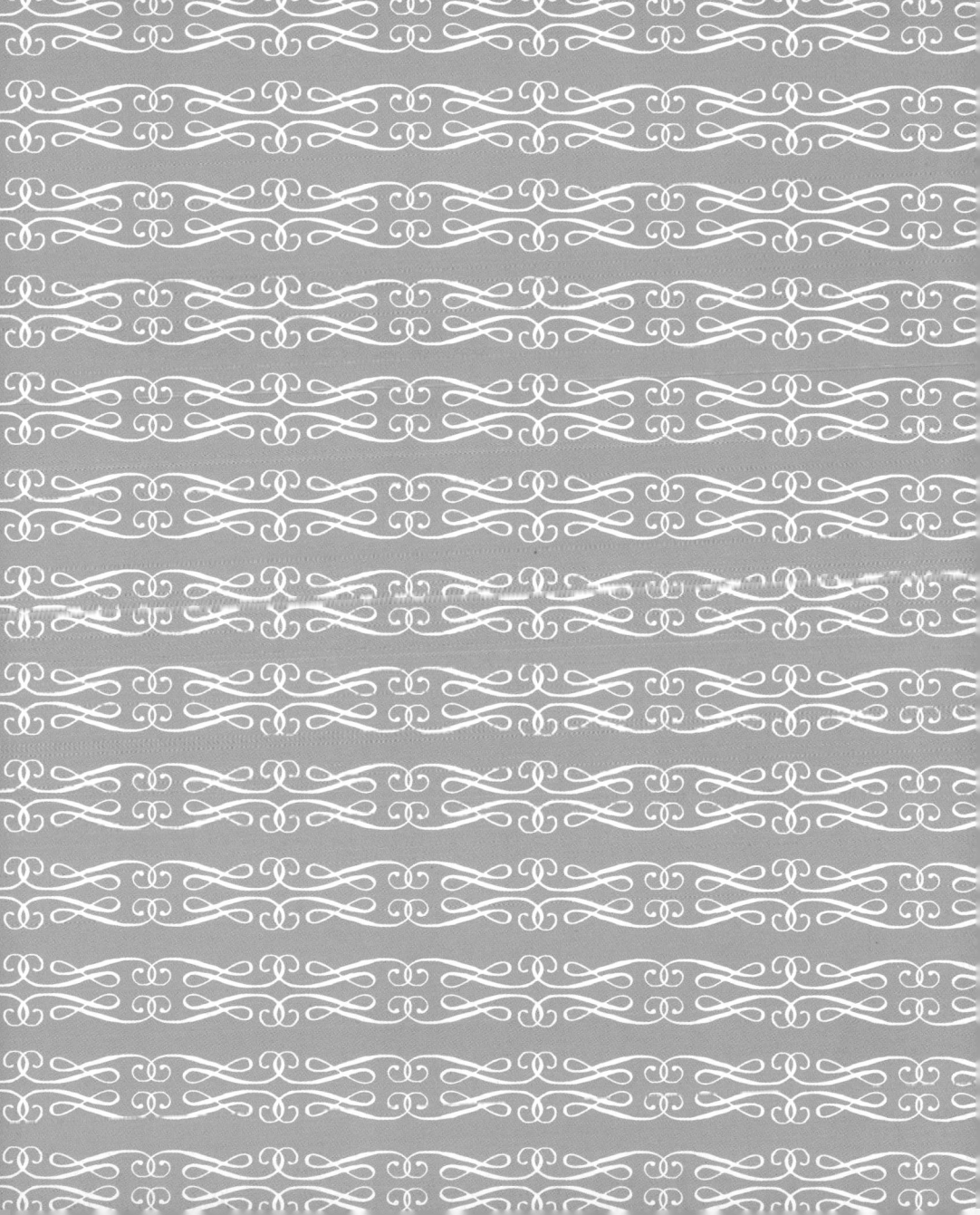

EMILY DOGINSON

Emily Doginson, a skittish saluki mix, loved to spy on passersby from the front window of her family's luxurious digs in Scramherst, Massachusetts. When visitors rang the doorbell, shy Emily retreated to her crate, refusing to emerge except for choice bits of chopped liver. Paper-trained from an early age, she wrote copious letters to the world, most of which were returned for insufficient postage. Ultimately, she selected her own society, then shut the doggy door.

I HEARD A DUCK QUACK

I heard a duck quack in the park;
I held my sit and stay.
A squirrel made whoopee with his nuts;
I turned my gaze away.

A flock of starlings flashed their wings;
They rose into the air,
Unreachable—then at my feet
There interloped a hare.

With moist, incautious, quaking jowls,
I watched that rabbit hop;
And then its whiskers twitched, and then
I could not stop to stop.

SKUNK IS THE THING *with* STINK BOMBS

Skunk is the thing with stink bombs

That leads a merry chase,

Then turns around and flicks its tail

And squirts me in the face.

Bath is the thing with soapsuds

And water cold as ice.

I wonder as I'm shivering,

Why was I hoodwinked twice?

WALT WHIPPET

Born in New Yorkie City, Walt Whippet was the everydog of his generation. An optimistic wag who saw the bowl as half full, he virtually never stopped vocalizing, even while asleep. Although critics have lambasted Whippet's rambling style, his faithful friend Arf Waldo Emerson hailed him as "a barking genius."

SONG *of* ME

—⊰⊱⊰⊱⊰—

I am Walt Whippet, white of muzzle and gay of tail, superior specimen of unsurpassed swiftness in the canine kingdom.

I bark of all things digestible and all things non-digestible.

I bark of the stomach dyspeptic.

I bark of bones ancient and bones new, bones pristine and bones masticated, rubber bones, nylabones, bones disguised as biscuits, and biscuits disguised as bones.

I draw nourishment from their marrow as I gnaw upon the mysteries of life.

I bark of liver biscotti, of turkey, chicken, and duck,

Of succulent morsels of meat beneath the table,

Of fresh rolls of toilet paper waiting to be unfurled.

I bark of snow, of rain and wind, of sleet and hail, of sun and moon,

Of shadows seen and unseen, of the surreptitious feline, the psychotic squirrel, the peripatetic pigeon.

I bark of holes in the ground and of holes not in the ground.

I bark of hats, both with heads and without heads.

I bark of firecrackers, sirens, the cello string plucked in the night, and of doorbells, both rung and unrung.

I bark of fences that carry an electrical charge and of all that may curtail the thrill of a day's adventure.

I bark of what the nose knows and of what the nose knows not,

Of the moist scent of crotches and other olfactory delights both complex and multitudinous.

I bark of all which is on the firmament, above and below the firmament, and in the great Sniffatorium beyond.

I bark of interminable poetic verses I know not how to end.

RUDYARD KIBBLE

Rudyard Kibble spent his youth jumping the fence in search of adventure. His owners were not amused when he returned home covered in cockleburs, reeking of skunk, or with a rear end full of BBs, so they put him to work learning obedience, agility, and herding.

No one was more surprised than Kibble himself when he collected dozens of blue ribbons for his efforts, shredding the odd red and yellow one along the way. Kibble, whose voracious appetite extended to fine literature, once memorized Elizabeth Basset Browning's *Sonnets from the Portuguese Water Dog* in less than an hour, while maintaining a perfect down/stay.

IF

If you can stare at dirt while all around you

 The other dogs keep working 'til they're through;

If you can break your stay when master trains you—

 Where heeling is concerned, you have no clue;

You leap the fence and gallop past your master

 Because a strutting pigeon caught your eye;

You take a shortcut home to get there faster,

 But, once you're there, cannot remember why;

If you can start your meal but stop your chewing

 To chase a garter snake into the ditch,

Or cock your head to hear what crows are doing,

 Or note the way the mouse's whiskers twitch;

If you abandon sheep you should have guarded,

    To chase the chickens halfway 'round the earth,

And daily vow such habits you've discarded,

    Yet find reform more trouble than it's worth;

If, on this list, you recognize your actions,

    Yet never have you tried to change, my lad,

Or ever stopped to ponder your infractions,

    Or noticed traits you share with dear old dad;

If you can take a simple task and blow it—

    And I believe that YES, indeed you CAN!—

Your birthright is this porch and all below it,

    For, son, you've got my short attention sp . . .

ROVER FROST

A four-time winner of the Poolitzer Prize, Rover Frost spent his life on working farms in the states of Vermont and New Rompshire. Though deceptively simple in theme, Frost's poetry is nothing to sniff at. Frost knew how to dig deep and had the dirt under his toenails to prove it. When asked why he so often wrote about flowers and insects, Frost replied, "because they taste good," and, when similarly questioned about his poetic obsession with trees, Frost explained that "their bark intrigues me."

SIZING UP SHOES ON A SOULFUL EVENING

Whose shoes these are you bet I know,

Size sixes, with a pointy toe.

The girl abandoned them in haste,

Beside the step two days ago.

Although they're far too tightly laced,

With tongues too tough to suit my taste,

The leather parts are soft, it's true;

I shall not let them go to waste.

It won't take long to munch these two,

Though I have three more pairs to chew,

And socks to boot before I spew,

And socks to boot before I spew.

NOSE

A nose is a nose,

And was always a nose.

And a dog licks his nose

When the nose overflows,

And the slicker it grows,

'Til it glistens and glows.

You can bet your sweet toes,

Nothing's nice as a nose,

Unless it's a tongue,

Or a tail, I suppose.

SNARL SANDBURG

An adventurous golden Labrador, Snarl Sandburg often ran away from his suburban home to roam the streets of Chicago, slurping up spilt milk and horse dung with equal enthusiasm.

Through hard work, Sandburg became a West Pointer, much to the chagrin of his mother, who insisted that pointing was not polite. Of humble beginnings, he often boasted that he never forgot where he came from, which was mostly true until the night he got spooked by the blast of a trumpet from a jazz bar, struck his head on a lamppost, and arrived home three days later in a fog he claimed "came on little cat feet."

PET-GO

Purveyor of Premium Pet Products,

Hamster Hustler, Pellet Pusher,

Peddler of Parakeets and the

Best Doggone Retail Outlet in Chi-Town:

You tell me it is overpriced and I believe you, but what is money for if not to provide everything your companion animal needs to lead a long and happy life.

And you tell me it is understaffed and I answer: Yes, it is true we have waited in line behind tap dancing turtles and irate iguanas, but what about the free biscuit the checkout lady always gives me, extra crunchy with no artificial additives.

And you tell me it is unsanitary and my reply is: Over on aisle four lives a cadre of cockroaches who have poked a hole in a carton of kibble, allowing me to munch first the one and then the other as I casually stroll by on my super durable flexi-lead.

And, having answered so, I add: Where else can one find a remote control raccoon with glow-in-the-dark eyes for a low $49.99, in a buy-one-get-one-free sale that runs through Labor Day.

Come and show me another store that offers chicken sweaters, mouse makeup, rabbit race cars and snake sandals;

Slithering

Squawking

Spewing

Stocking, selling, reselling,

A wide assortment of guppy umbrellas! Proud to be the Purveyor of Premium Pet Products, Hamster Hustler, Pellet Pusher, Parakeet Peddler and Best Doggone Retail Outlet in Chi-Town.

WILLIAM CORGI WILLIAMS

Despite the stubby legs characteristic of his breed, Williams rose to great heights as a poet. In his youth, he attended Bark Twain School for Scamps, where he ran in a pack with Ezra Hound and P. P. Cummings. In his later years, Williams suffered prolonged bouts of nausea, aggravated by eating too many stolen plums.

OH,  BY THE WAY

I have gobbled
the bratwurst
you left on
the counter,

the fries,
the kosher pickle,
and two-ply
napkin

then threw them
all up
on the new rug
in the foyer.

Forgive me,
but was white
a wise
choice of colors?

 RED FIRE HYDRANT

so much depends

upon

a red fire

hydrant

gleaming

in the sun

beside the relieved

Dalmatians.

DOROTHY BARKER

A Yorkshire terrier, Dorothy Barker was born in a dilapidated tractor shed in Pugkeepsie, New York, the runt of the litter. Notoriously quick of tongue, Ms. Barker had multiple bones to pick about domesticated life, including pet shop politics, the overpopulation of the urban squirrel, and the lack of sophisticated clothes for the toy breeds. Today the pint-size poet is best remembered for her biting wit.

DISILLUSIONMENT

My health fell apart

When I met a Maltese.

I gave him my heart.

He gave me his fleas.

ESTRUS

"You're in heat," my owners told me,
And I promptly let them know
They can call me names or scold me,
I'm not going with the flow!
All these pheromones confuse me,
And I've missed a dozen naps
Due to panties that bemuse me
With their ruffles, bows and snaps.
My condition must be chronic
(It will last three weeks, I'm told.)
And I find it quite ironic:
My first heat leaves me cold.

BRED

As far as being mated,

It is highly overrated.

LACTATION

Each pregnancy, labor and birth,

Have impacted my teats and my girth.

Now I make all my pups drink from cartons and cups,

'Cause they've milked me for all I am worth.

P. P. CUMMINGS

The joy of urination is a recurrent theme in the poetry, plays, and paintings of P. P. Cummings, who enjoyed capitalizing on the wordplay of his initials.

Claiming dalmatian ancestry, Cummings made spotty punctuation his trademark. To this day, no one has the slightest idea what his words of whizdom mean, prompting critics to dismiss his work as being "all wet."

ANYDOG LIVED IN A BOWWOW HOUSE

anydog lived in a bowwow house

with schnoodle guinea pig lovebird mouse

lick by muzzle and twitch by dream

he sniffed his fluffies he whizzed his stream

schnoodle and anydog scruffyandspot

trotted one day to a vacant lot

fetch by frisbee and toy by squeak

they ran their zoomies they growled their speak.

anydog strayed to a hot wire fence

(lift leg aim fire dumb by dense)

anydog's Winkie most magical thing

yip yap howl yowl zip zap zing

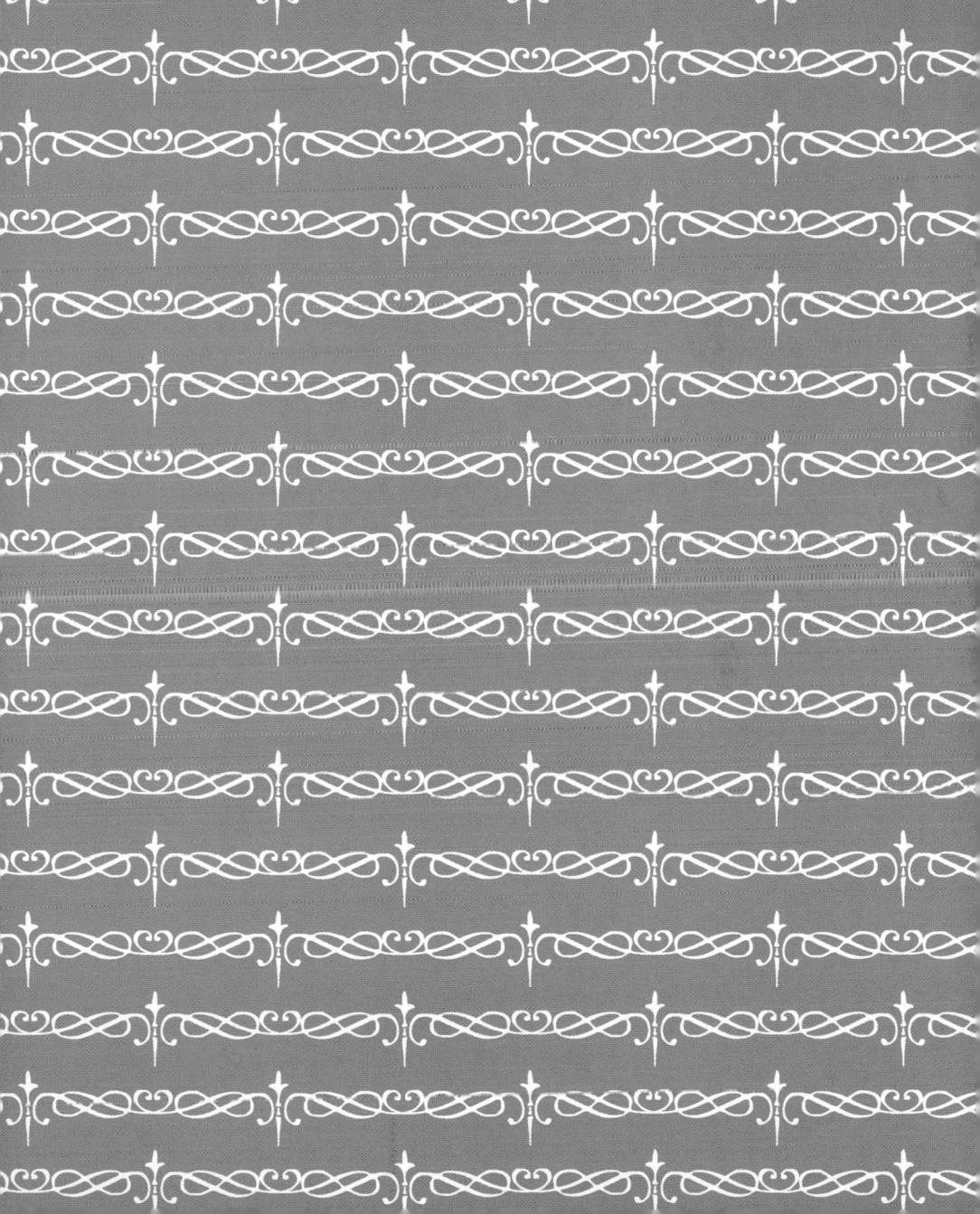

DROOLIN' THOMAS

Droolin' Thomas was born in the land of Whales. Growing up, the curly-coated poet often claimed to feel "like a fish out of water," which may account for why his sense of humor was so dry.

Plagued by hypersalivation, Thomas endured muzzles and other crude forms of orthodog-ture in a desperate attempt to staunch the flow. "I can stop any time I want to," Thomas said of his drooling problem, which was second only to his lying problem. Right up until the end, his creative spirit remained undampened, although chronic insomnia made him one cranky SOB.

DO NOT ANNOY ME  YOUR
CONSTANT YAP

Do not annoy me with your constant yap,

Old dogs should dream and doze throughout the day;

Please, please shut up so I can take a nap.

Glib girls who gush such sentimental sap,

Whimpering woe which wafts from blocks away,

Do not annoy me with your constant yap.

Brash girls with phones who let their pierced tongues flap

Assault my ears with nasty words they say,

Please, please shut up so I can take a nap.

Shrill girls with flying fingers wave and clap

And thunder shriek woo-hoo and whoop hooray,

Do not annoy me with your constant yap.

Mad girls, red-faced, who rant and stomp and slap,

Exuding wrath to fight the fiddling fray,

Please, please shut up so I can take a nap.

And you, girl, twang the banjo on your lap,

While down the hall more bad musicians play.

Do not annoy me with your constant yap.

Please, please shut up so I can take a nap.

DOGDEN DASH

A sad-eyed bluetick coonhound, Dogden Dash spent his puppyhood barking up the wrong tree. On his first day of obedience school, the high-spirited wag was expelled for mounting Dorothy Barker, who turned around and bit him where it hurt. Dash, who possessed a keen nose for satire, is famous for his use of the rhymed puplet.

HOW TO AVOID GETTING
OTTERITIS

Never tease a weasel,

He is meaner than a mink,

He is hotter than an otter,

He's a skunk without the stink.

Of the genus called *Mustela*,

He's got pointy teeth, this fella,

And his relatives are vermin,

Wrapped in stoats of Ethel Ermine.

Don't appease a weasel

With a hug around his knees,

For that's the very quickest way

To make a weasel wease.

Never squeeze a weasel
If the weasel's partly squoze,
For he'll launch a full repreasel
That you'll pay for through the nose.

You will get a grave diseasel
If you seize him by the throat,
Otteritis or the measel,
End of subject, quote, unquote.

SPECIAL DELIVERY

Judging by their ankles, here's my educated guess:

The FedEx man tastes better than the guy from UPS.

DEAR DECEASED DALMATIAN

Although you're gone, it's no surprise,

We still see spots before our eyes.

COCK-A-DOODLE-DON'T

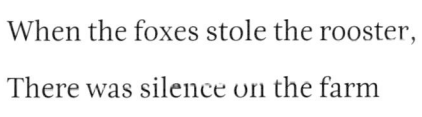

When the foxes stole the rooster,

There was silence on the farm

'Til the happy hens replaced him

With a digital alarm.

RATS

They met a cat they both befriended.

That is where their story ended.

ONE-WAY TICKET

There once was a greyhound named Gus,

Who reached heaven with minimal fuss.

Said his practical pastor,

"He'd have gotten there faster

If he'd just hitched a ride on the bus."

TIME OUT

The turkey, the hen, the gander and goose

Went out to the ice rink one day.

When a nearsighted duck hit the hen with a puck,

The police wrote it up as "fowl play."

ANONYMUTT

Who is the prolific poet called Anonymutt? Some believe him or her to be a single individual piddling with multiple poetic forms. Others maintain that the mysterious *nom de plume* represents a collective of backyard bards determined to keep their identities in the doghouse.

Despite the uneven quality of his/her/their work, Anonymutt has undoubtedly enriched canine literature by leaving piles of verses all across the globe.

ODE TO P. P. CUMMINGS

He's a poet and a painter,

With a style that's bold and free.

The cityscape's his canvas,

And his medium is pee.

In vacant lots, on grassy plots,

On sidewalks, trees, and dirt,

He'll dribble, drizzle, tinkle,

Sprinkle, urinate, and squirt.

His specialty is fluid designs.
The connoisseurs agree,
His watercolors show
A flow of virtuosity.

Though every time he signs his name,
It gives him quite a rush,
His favorite part of making art
Is cleaning off his brush.

GOD MADE DOG

Way back in the beginning,

When the world was just a pup,

God studied his creation

As the morning sun came up.

Was Pig too pink? Giraffe too tall?

What changes should He make?

Already God was wondering

If Skunk was a mistake.

A vital piece was missing.

What in heaven could it be?

"I shall make my finest creature.

I shall call it D-O-G."

The angels gathered round Him
In the workshop of the Lord,
While God whipped up some sketches
On His holy drawing board.

Behold, He mixed a thundercloud
With wisps of ocean fog,
Made ears to flop and tail to wag,
And lo, the Lord made Dog!

"I'll call this dog the Greyhound.
It shall be my swiftest breed."
He touched its legs with lightning bolts
To give it extra speed.

Day two, God made the Labrador

And taught it to retrieve

An apple ripe for Adam's lunch

And garden tools for Eve.

With raisin dots and leopard spots

He made the bold Dalmatian,

And let it bark and leave its mark

All over His creation.

Day three, God made the Beagle

And the Dachshund low to ground,

The Bulldog and the Corgi

And the howling Basset Hound.

The Springer Spaniel sprang to life

And then the Irish Setter.

Hallelujah, praise the Lord,

Could Dog get any better?

Day four, He made Samoyed
From a drift of fallen snow,
And then a team of Huskies
With a silver sled to tow.

Day five, God made the Bloodhound
From a batch of crinkled clay,
Then tweaked the ears and squished the nose
For Pug and for Shar-Pei

The sixth day came the Pekingese,
Maltese, and Yorkshire Terrier.
(God's work was getting smaller now
And infinitely hairier.)

To use the clay left over,
Plus the whiskers, fur and paste,
(For in God's holy workshop
Nothing ever went to waste . . .)

He crafted the Chihuahua,

Very cute and *muy chiquito,*

Then scratched his head and sighed

And said, "Amen, I'm done, *finito.*"

But just for fun, when day was done,

He made the Chinese Crested.

Day seven, He was so dog-tired,

God should have stopped and rested . . .

. . . But lo, His wisdom faileth,

For instead of doing that,

He lost his ever-loving mind

And God created CAT.